Trace the nu

Big Book of Number Tracing: 0-100

Trace and write the number 0.

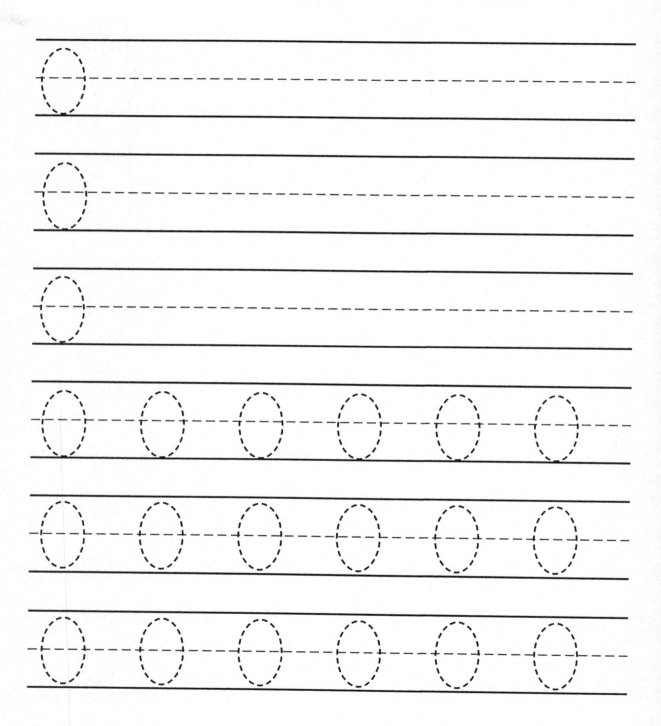

Big Book of Number Tracing: 0-100

Trace numbers 1-10.

1 1 1 1 1 1 1

2 2 2 2 2 2 2

3 3 3 3 3 3 3

4 4 4 4 4 4 4

5 5 5 5 5 5 5

6 6 6 6 6 6 6

Big Book of Number Tracing: 0-100

Trace numbers 1-10.

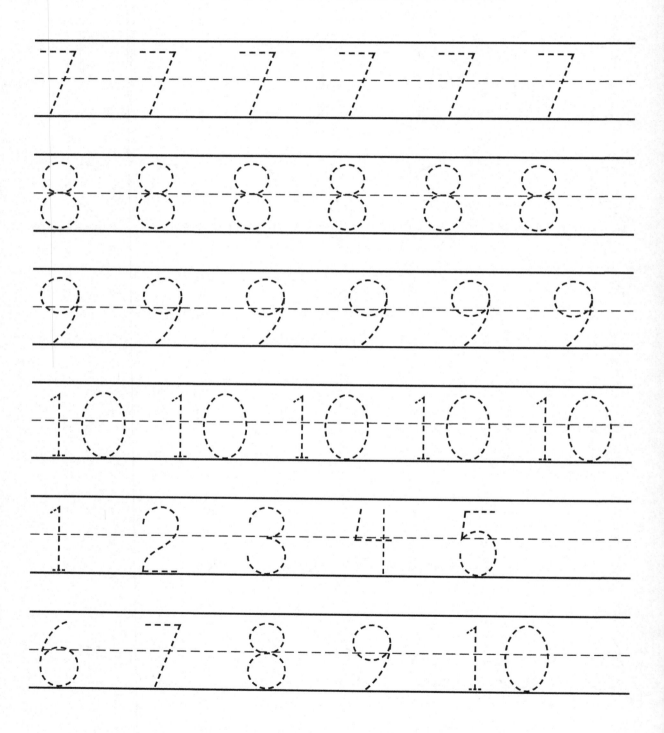

Big Book of Number Tracing: 0-100

Practice writing numbers 1-10.

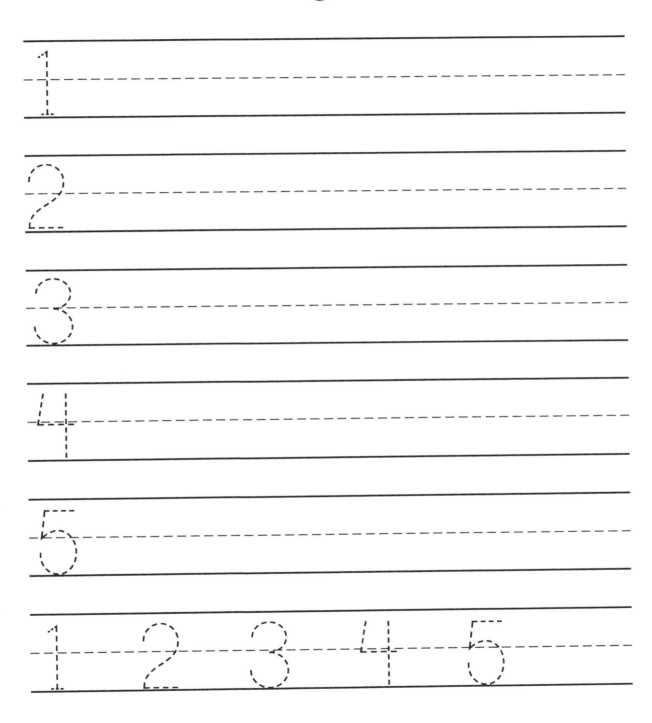

Big Book of Number Tracing: 0-100

Practice writing numbers 1-10.

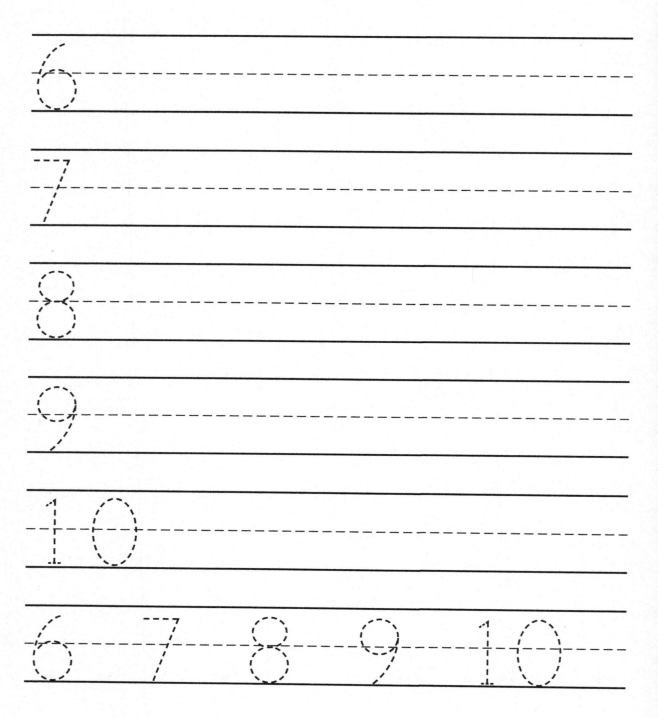

Big Book of Number Tracing: 0-100

Trace numbers 11-20.

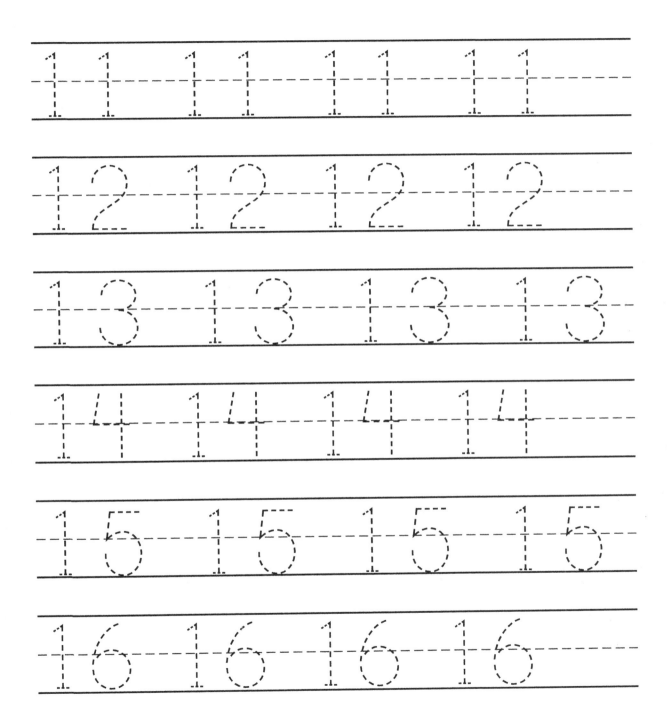

Big Book of Number Tracing: 0-100

Trace numbers 11-20.

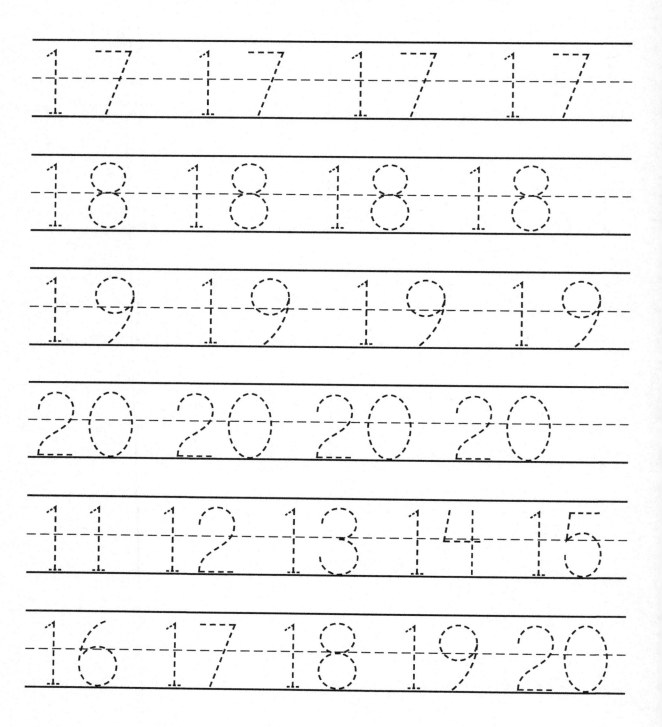

Big Book of Number Tracing: 0-100

Practice writing numbers 11-20.

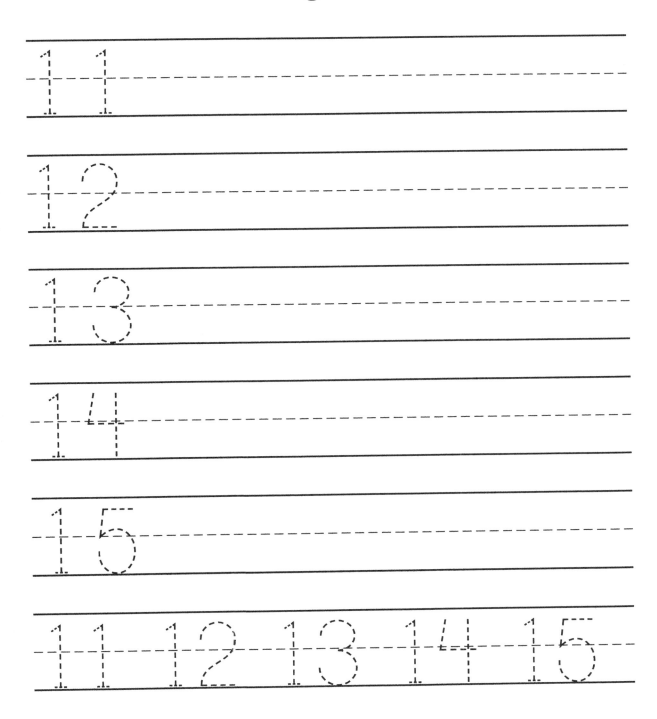

Big Book of Number Tracing: 0-100

Practice writing numbers 11-20.

Big Book of Number Tracing: 0-100

Trace numbers 21-30.

21 21 21 21 21

22 22 22 22 22

23 23 23 23 23

24 24 24 24 24

25 25 25 25 25

26 26 26 26 26

Trace numbers 21-30.

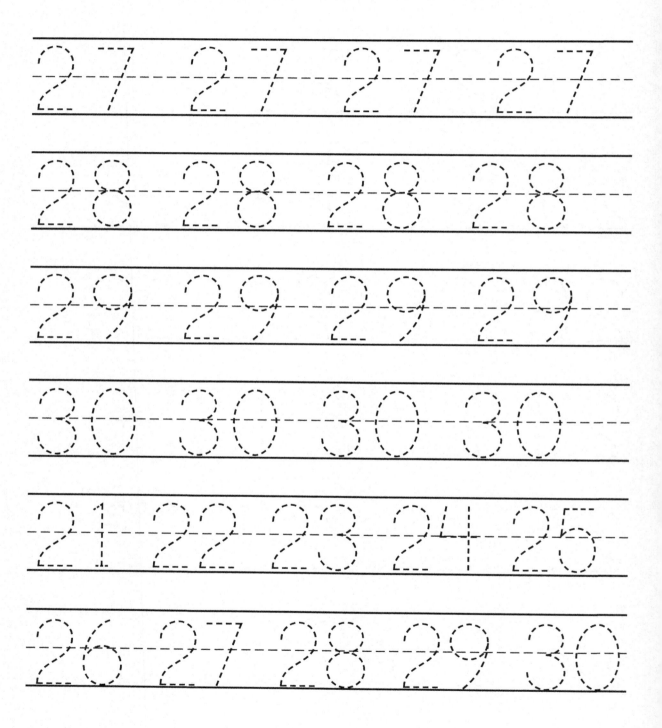

Big Book of Number Tracing: 0-100

Practice writing numbers 21-30.

Big Book of Number Tracing: 0-100

Practice writing numbers 21-30.

26

27

28

29

30

26 27 28 29 30

Big Book of Number Tracing: 0-100

Trace numbers 31-40.

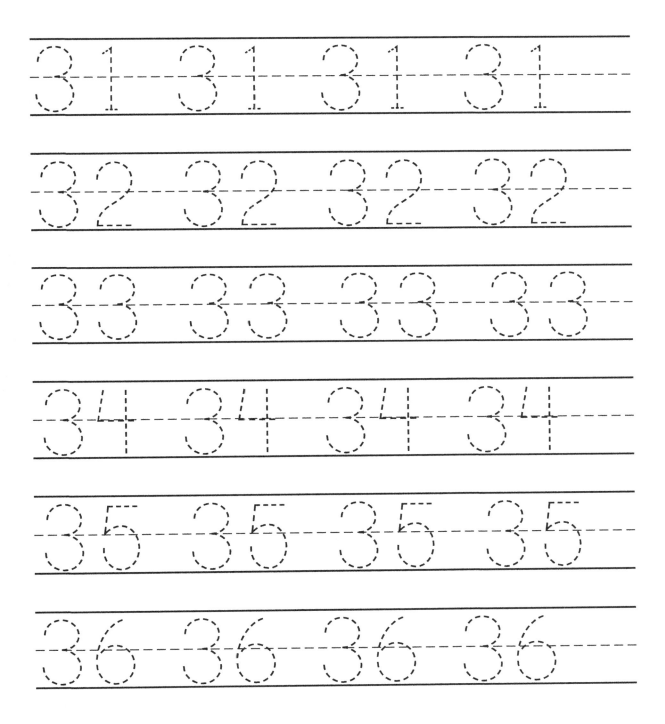

Big Book of Number Tracing: 0-100

Trace numbers 31-40.

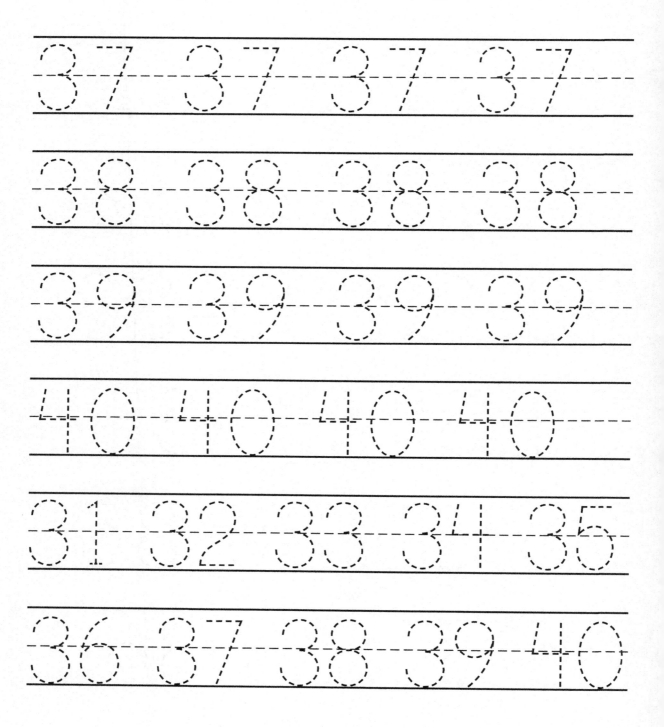

Big Book of Number Tracing: 0-100

Practice writing numbers 31-40.

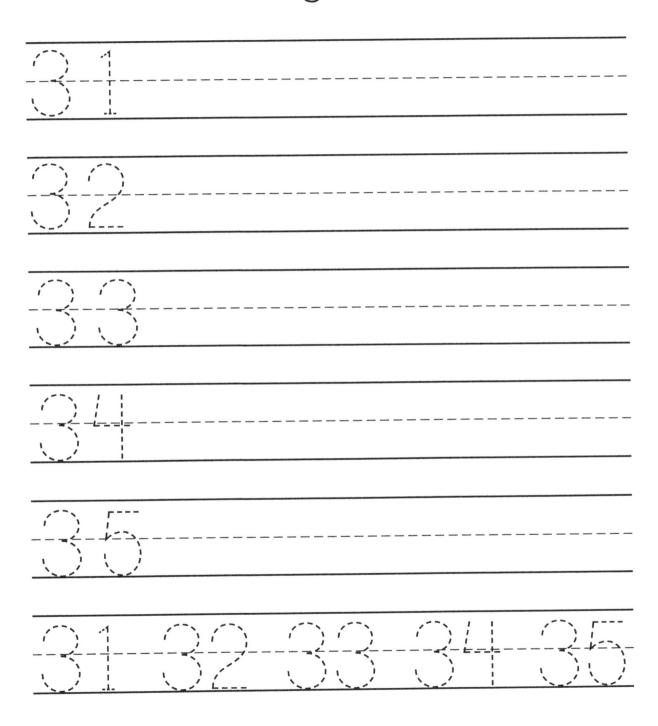

Big Book of Number Tracing: 0-100

Practice writing numbers 31-40.

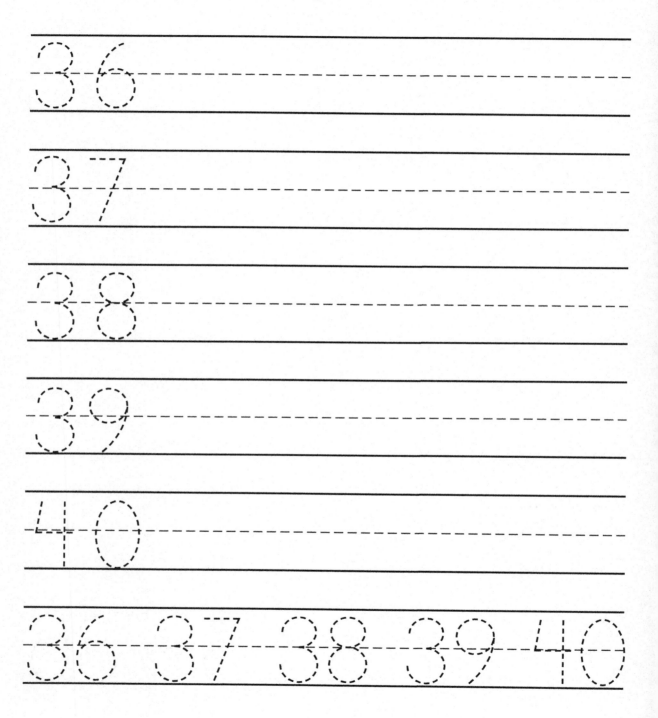

Big Book of Number Tracing: 0-100

Trace numbers 41-50.

41 41 41 41

42 42 42 42

43 43 43 43

44 44 44 44

45 45 45 45

46 46 46 46

Big Book of Number Tracing: 0-100

Trace numbers 41-50.

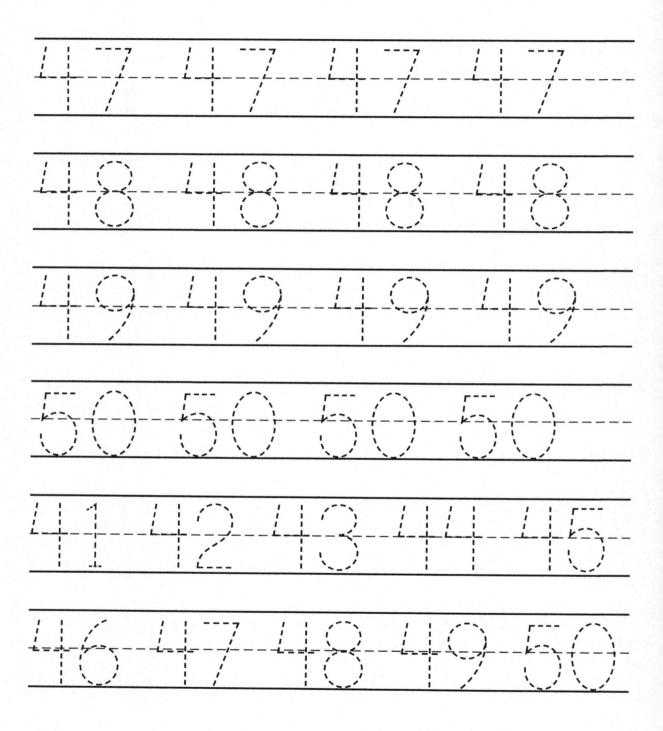

Big Book of Number Tracing: 0-100

Practice writing numbers 41-50.

Big Book of Number Tracing: 0-100

Practice writing numbers 41-50.

Big Book of Number Tracing: 0-100

Practice Review 1-50.

Big Book of Number Tracing: 0-100

Practice Review 1-50.

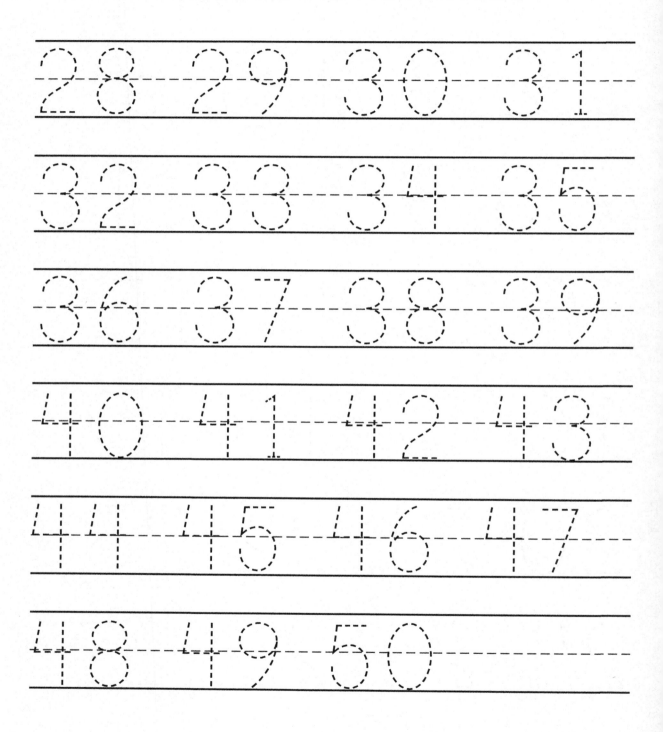

Big Book of Number Tracing: 0-100

Trace numbers 51-60.

51 51 51 51 51

52 52 52 52 52

53 53 53 53 53

54 54 54 54 54

55 55 55 55 55

56 56 56 56 56

Big Book of Number Tracing: 0-100

Trace numbers 51-60.

57 57 57 57

58 58 58 58

59 59 59 59

60 60 60 60

51 52 53 54 55

56 57 58 59 60

Big Book of Number Tracing: 0-100

Practice writing numbers 51-60.

51

52

53

54

55

51 52 53 54 55

Big Book of Number Tracing: 0-100

Practice writing numbers 51-60.

56

57

58

59

60

56 57 58 59 60

Big Book of Number Tracing: 0-100

Trace numbers 61-70.

61 61 61 61

62 62 62 62

63 63 63 63

64 64 64 64

65 65 65 65

66 66 66 66

Big Book of Number Tracing: 0-100

Trace numbers 61-70.

Big Book of Number Tracing: 0-100

Practice writing numbers 61-70.

Big Book of Number Tracing: 0-100

Practice writing numbers 61-70.

Big Book of Number Tracing: 0-100

Trace numbers 71-80.

71 71 71 71 71

72 72 72 72 72

73 73 73 73 73

74 74 74 74 74

75 75 75 75 75

76 76 76 76 76

Big Book of Number Tracing: 0-100

Trace numbers 71-80.

Big Book of Number Tracing: 0-100

Practice writing numbers 71-80.

Big Book of Number Tracing: 0-100

Practice writing numbers 71-80.

76

77

78

79

80

76 77 78 79 80

Big Book of Number Tracing: 0-100

Trace numbers 81-90.

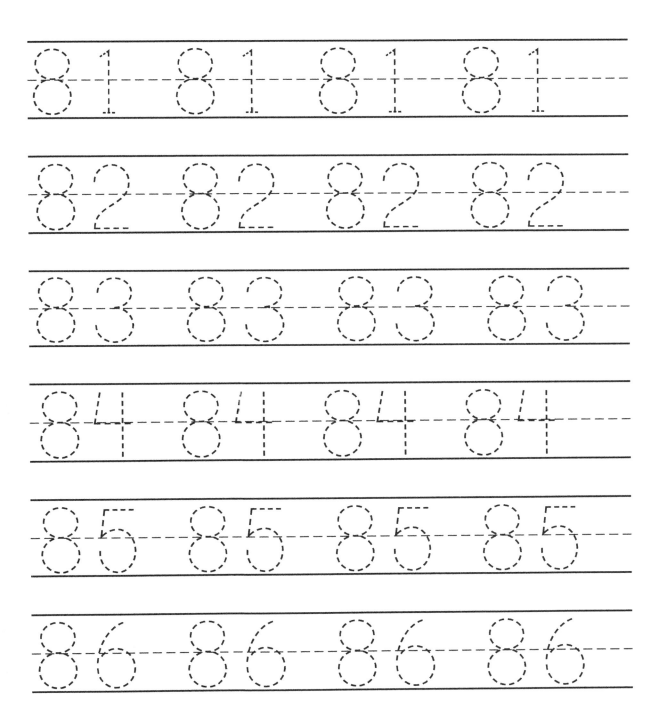

Big Book of Number Tracing: 0-100

Trace numbers 81-90.

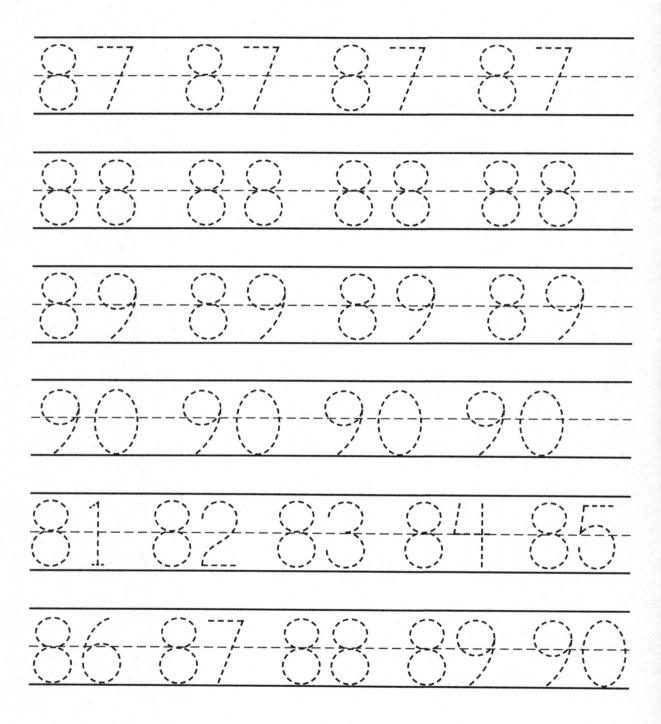

Big Book of Number Tracing: 0-100

Practice writing numbers 81-90.

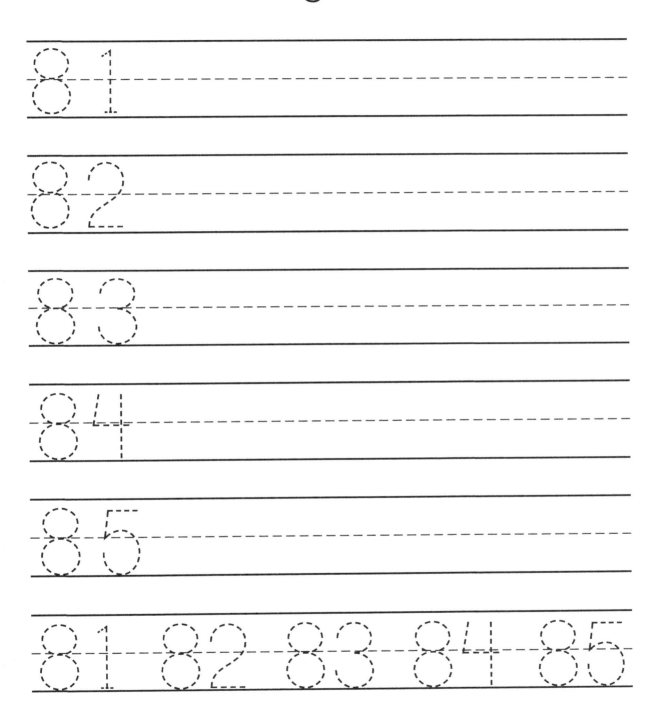

Big Book of Number Tracing: 0-100

Practice writing numbers 81-90.

86

87

88

89

90

86 87 88 89 90

Big Book of Number Tracing: 0-100

Trace numbers 91-100.

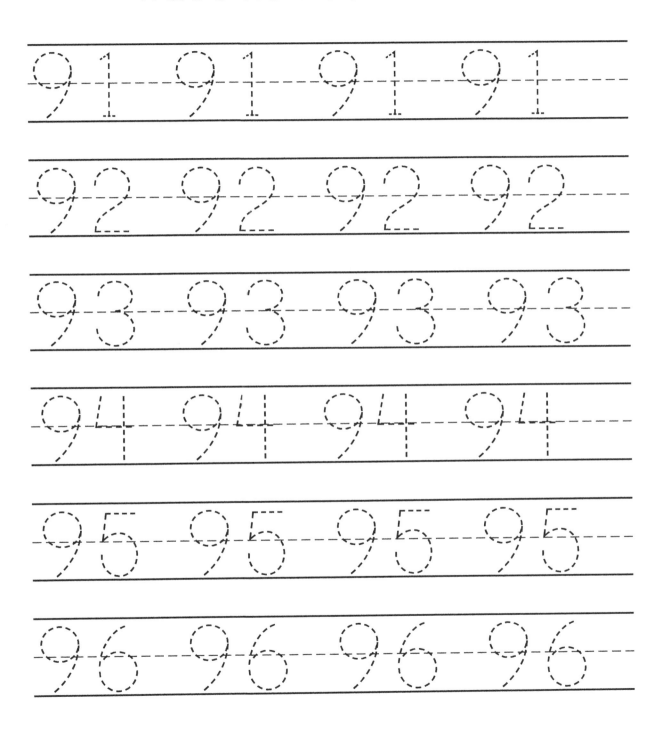

Big Book of Number Tracing: 0-100

Trace numbers 91-100.

97 97 97 97

98 98 98 98

99 99 99 99

100 100 100

91 92 93 94 95

96 97 98 99 100

Big Book of Number Tracing: 0-100

Practice writing numbers 91-100.

91 -----------------------------

92 -----------------------------

93 -----------------------------

94 -----------------------------

95 -----------------------------

91 92 93 94 95

Big Book of Number Tracing: 0-100

Practice writing numbers 91-100.

96

97

98

99

100

96 97 98 99 100

Big Book of Number Tracing: 0-100

Practice Review 51-100.

51 52 53 54

55 56 57 58

59 60 61 62

63 64 65 66

67 68 69 70

71 72 73 74 75

Big Book of Number Tracing: 0-100

Practice Review 51-100.

76 77 78 79

80 81 82 83

84 85 86 87

88 89 90 91

92 93 94 95

96 97 98 99 100

Big Book of Number Tracing: 0-100

Practice Review 0-100.

0 1 2 3 4 5 6

7 8 9 10 11

12 13 14 15

16 17 18 19

20 21 22 23

24 25 26 27

Big Book of Number Tracing: 0-100

Practice Review 0-100.

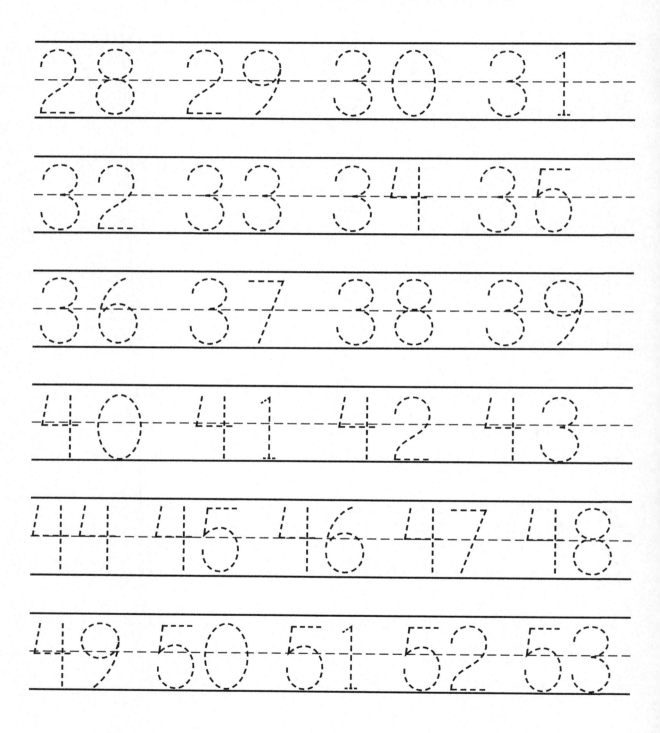

Big Book of Number Tracing: 0-100

Practice Review 0-100.

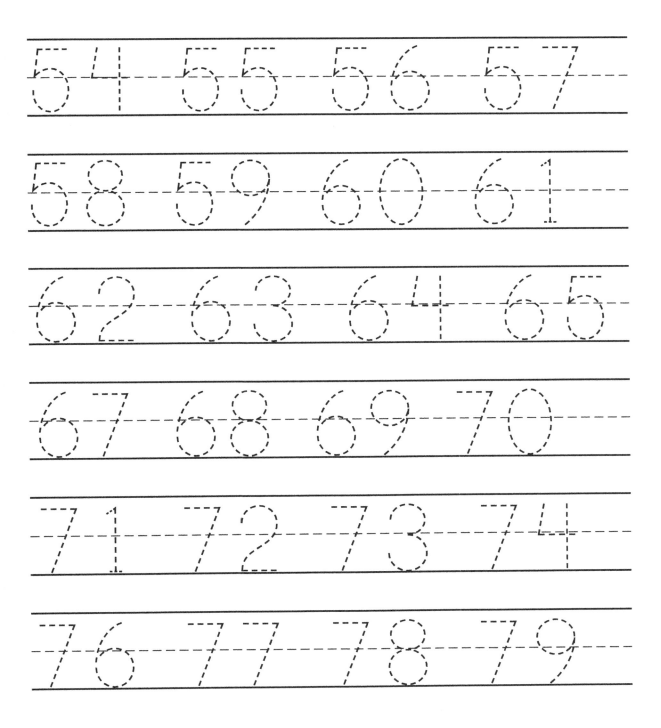

Big Book of Number Tracing: 0-100

Practice Review 0-100.

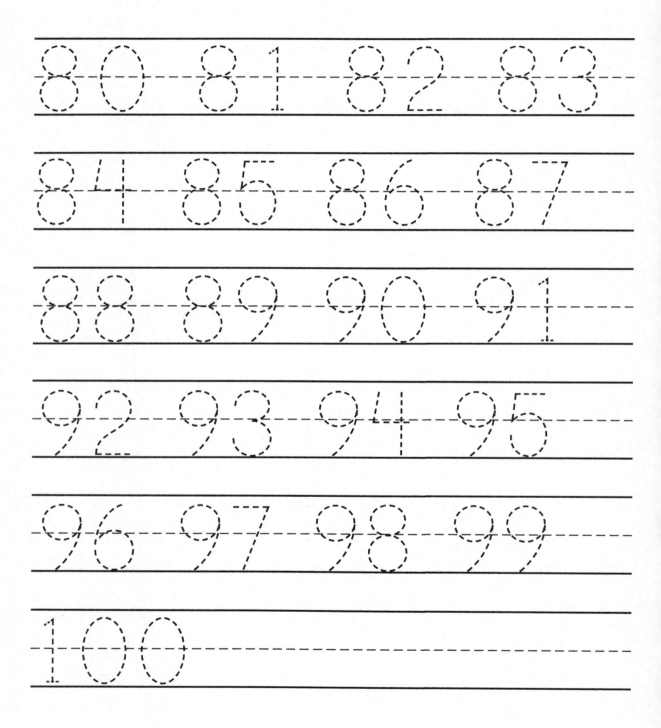

Big Book of Number Tracing: 0-100

Trace and write the number 0.

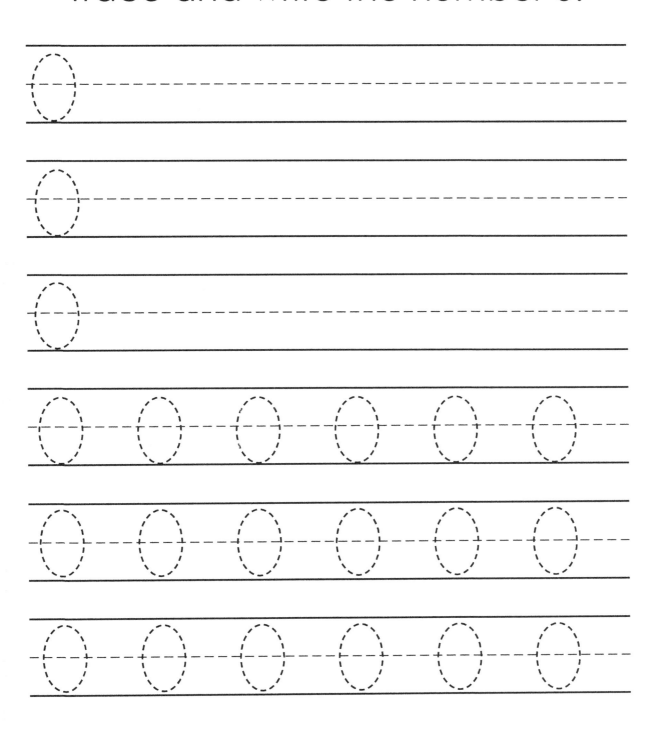

Big Book of Number Tracing: 0-100

Practice writing numbers 1-100.

Big Book of Number Tracing: 0-100

Practice writing numbers 1-100.

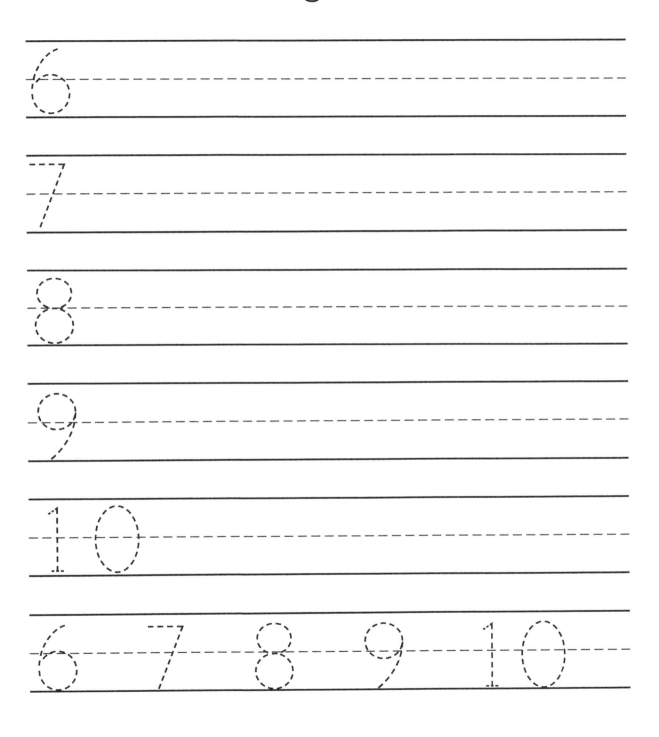

Big Book of Number Tracing: 0-100

Practice writing numbers 1-100.

Big Book of Number Tracing: 0-100

Practice writing numbers 1-100.

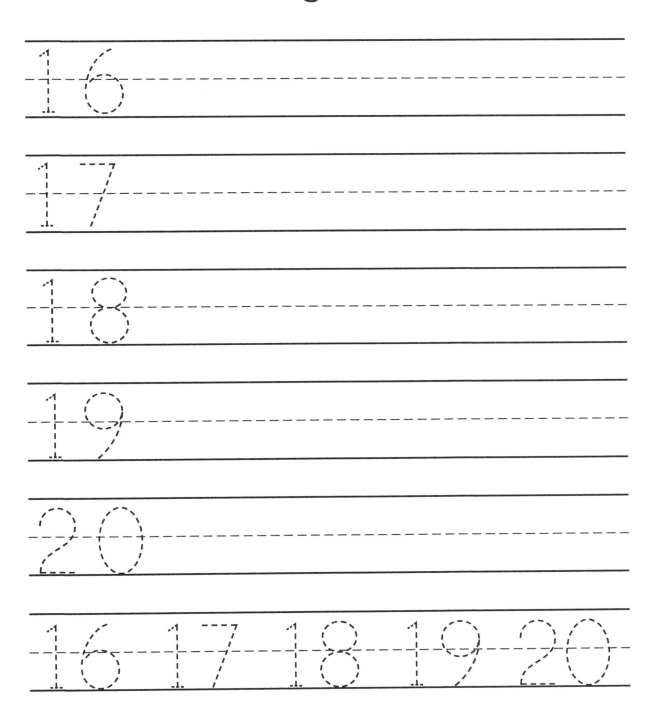

Big Book of Number Tracing: 0-100

Practice writing numbers 1-100.

21

22

23

24

25

21 22 23 24 25

Big Book of Number Tracing: 0-100

Practice writing numbers 1-100.

Big Book of Number Tracing: 0-100

Practice writing numbers 1-100.

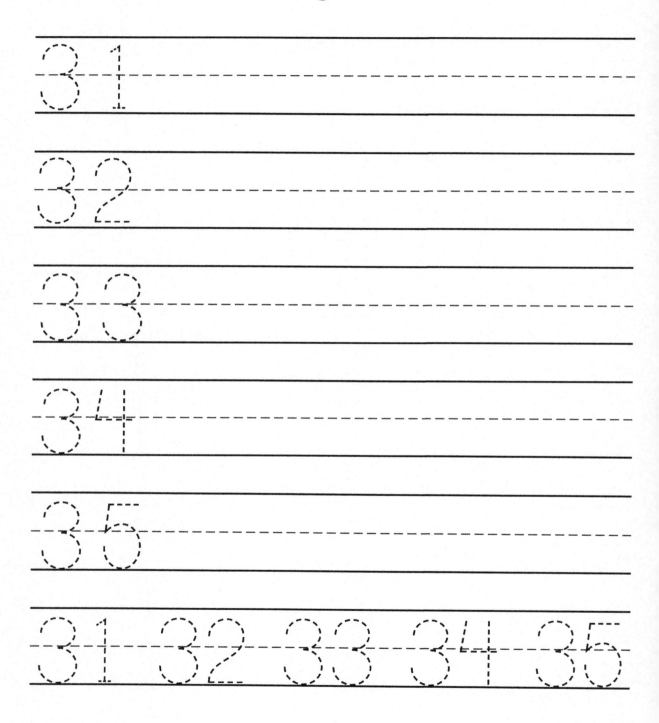

Big Book of Number Tracing: 0-100

Practice writing numbers 1-100.

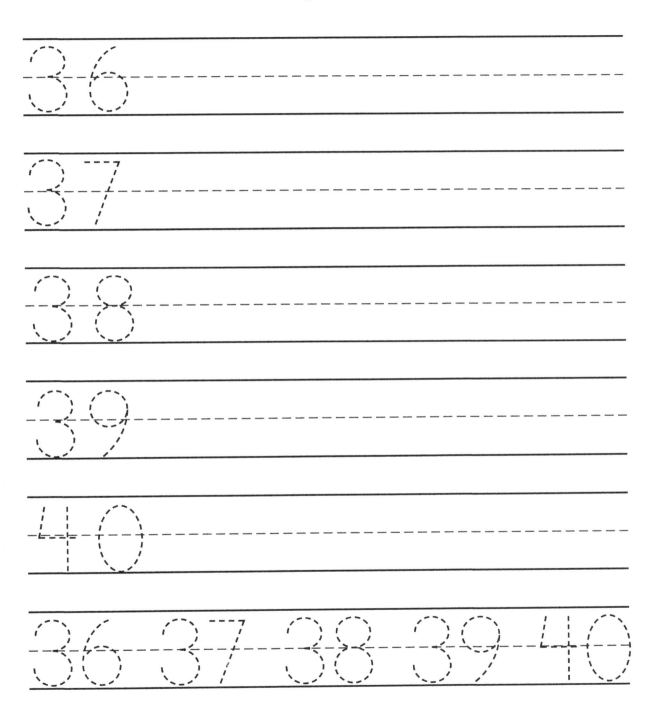

Big Book of Number Tracing: 0-100

Practice writing numbers 1-100.

41

42

43

44

45

41 42 43 44 45

Big Book of Number Tracing: 0-100

Practice writing numbers 1-100.

46

47

48

49

50

46 47 48 49 50

Big Book of Number Tracing: 0-100

Practice writing numbers 1-100.

51

52

53

54

55

51 52 53 54 55

Big Book of Number Tracing: 0-100

Practice writing numbers 1-100.

56

57

58

59

60

56 57 58 59 60

Big Book of Number Tracing: 0-100

Practice writing numbers 1-100.

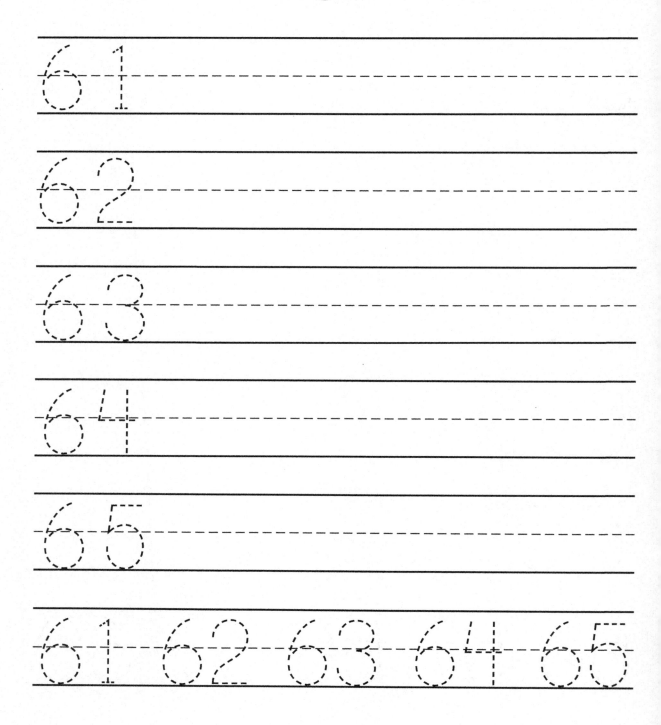

Big Book of Number Tracing: 0-100

Practice writing numbers 1-100.

Big Book of Number Tracing: 0-100

Practice writing numbers 1-100.

71

72

73

74

75

71 72 73 74 75

Big Book of Number Tracing: 0-100

Practice writing numbers 1-100.

Practice writing numbers 1-100.

81

82

83

84

85

81 82 83 84 85

Big Book of Number Tracing: 0-100

Practice writing numbers 1-100.

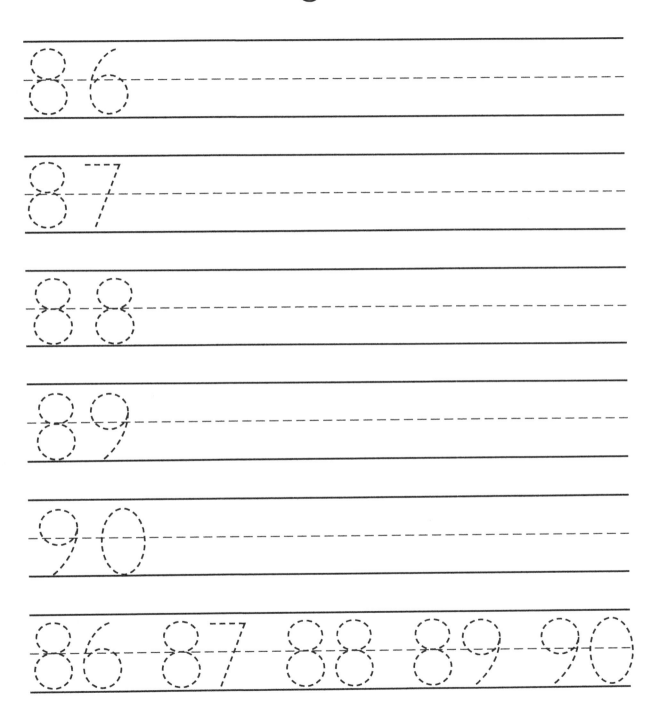

Big Book of Number Tracing: 0-100

Practice writing numbers 1-100.

91

92

93

94

95

91 92 93 94 95

Big Book of Number Tracing: 0-100

Practice writing numbers 1-100.

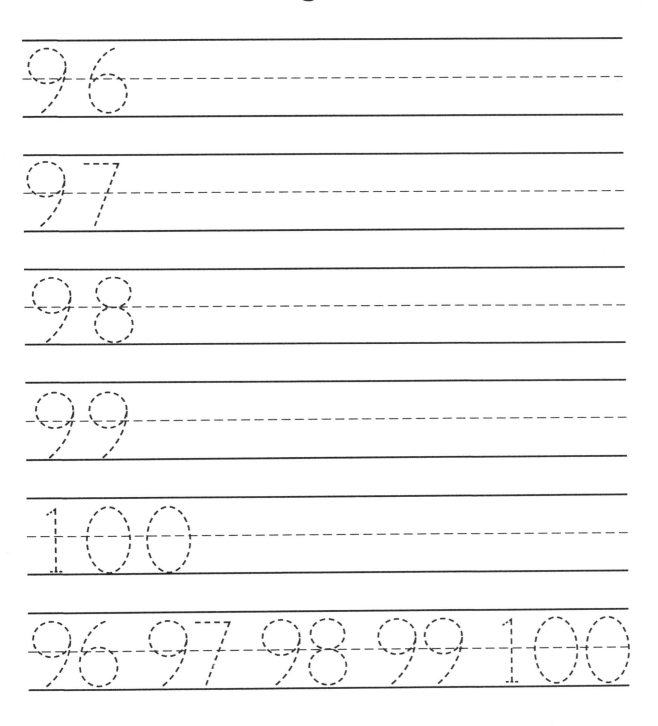

Big Book of Number Tracing: 0-100

Practice Review 0-100.

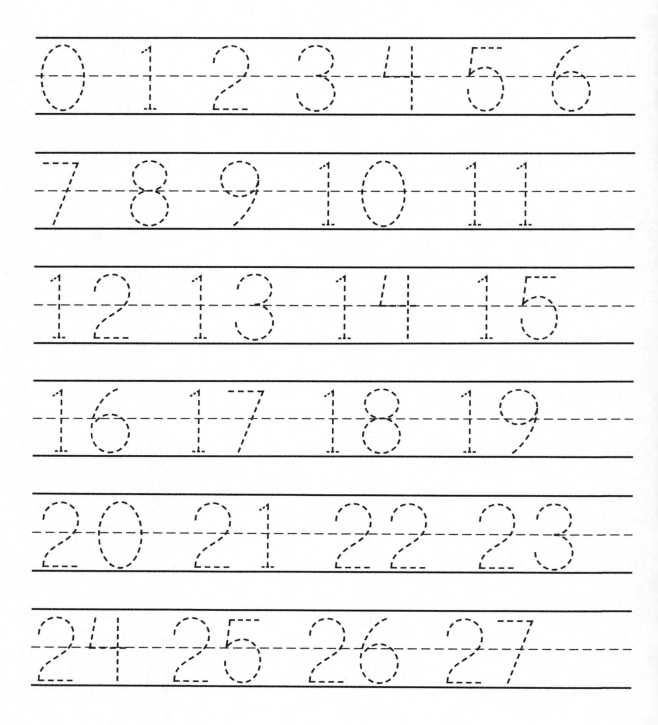

Big Book of Number Tracing: 0-100

Practice Review 0-100.

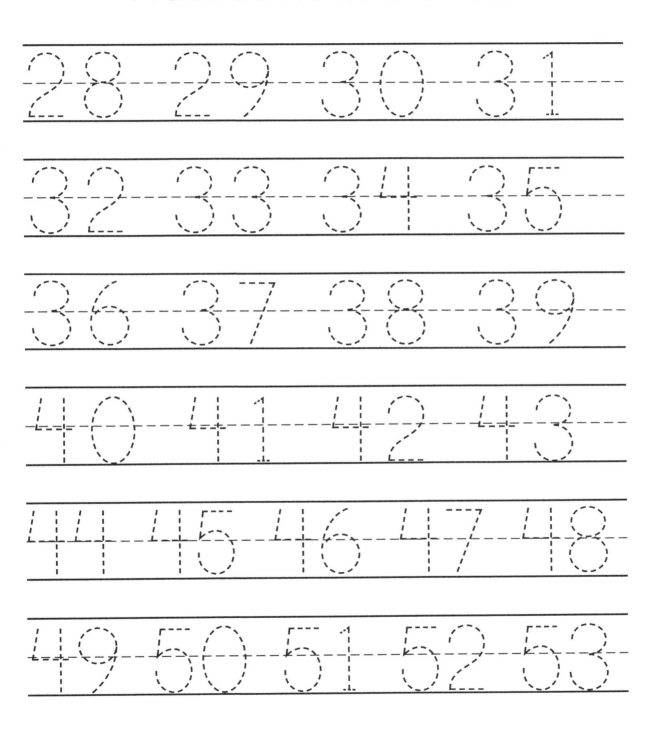

Big Book of Number Tracing: 0-100

Practice Review 0-100.

54 55 56 57

58 59 60 61

62 63 64 65

67 68 69 70

71 72 73 74

76 77 78 79

Big Book of Number Tracing: 0-100

Practice Review 0-100.

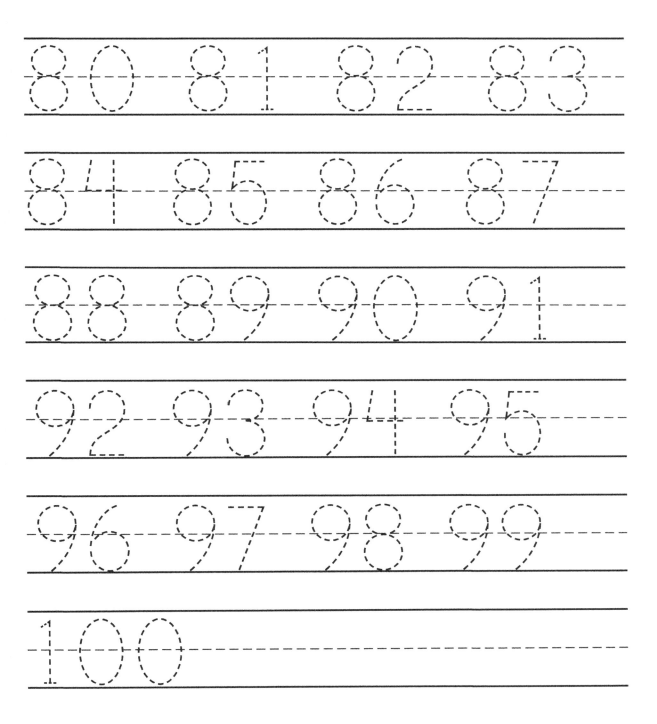

Big Book of Number Tracing: 0-100

Practice writing the number 0.

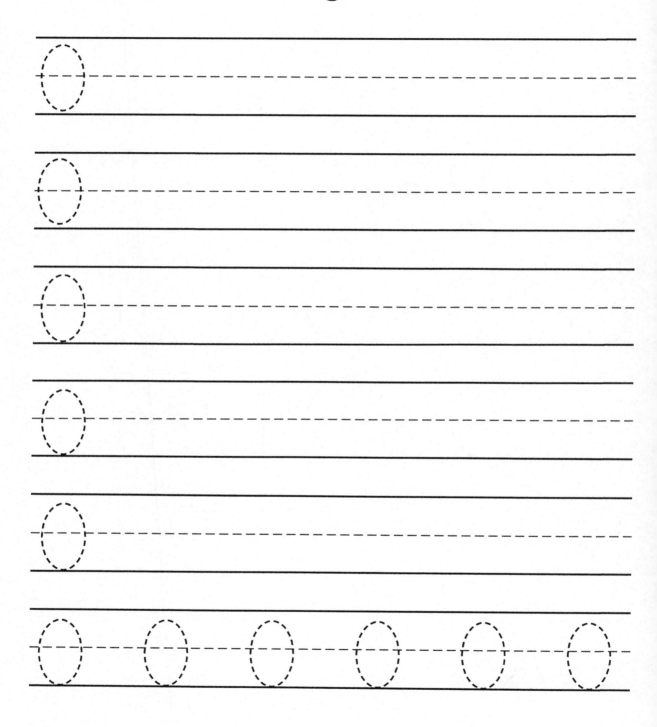

Big Book of Number Tracing: 0-100

Practice writing numbers 1-100.

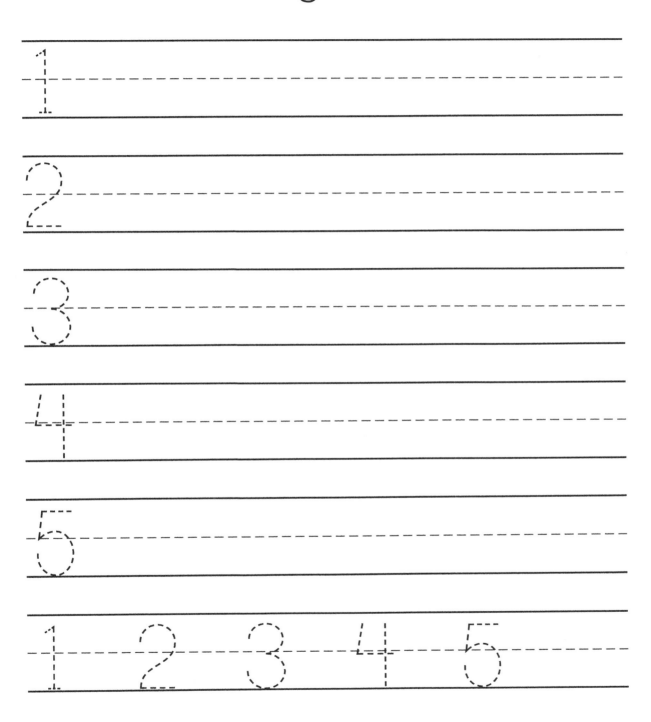

Big Book of Number Tracing: 0-100

Practice writing numbers 1-100.

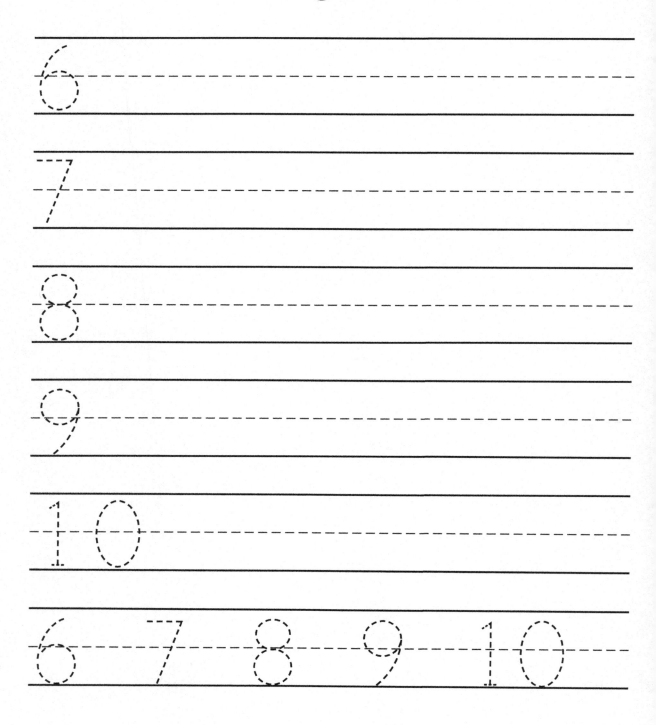

Big Book of Number Tracing: 0-100

Practice writing numbers 1-100.

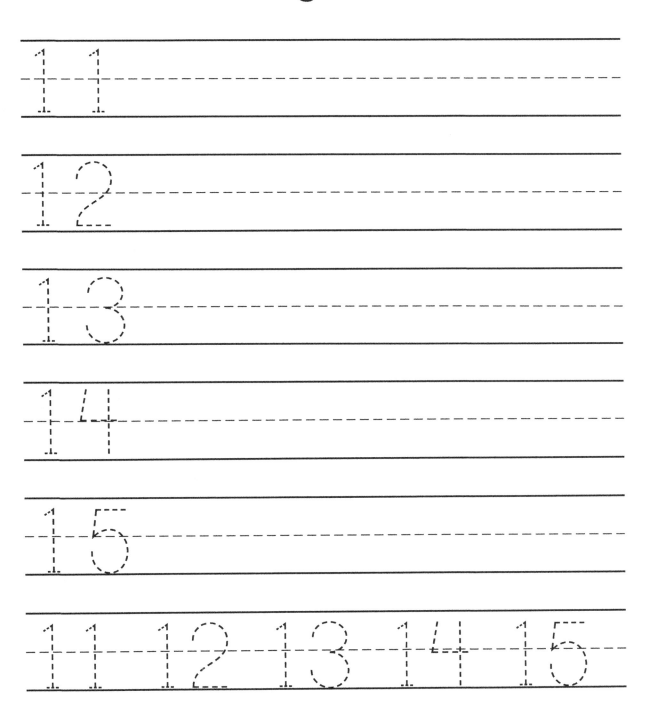

Big Book of Number Tracing: 0-100

Practice writing numbers 1-100.

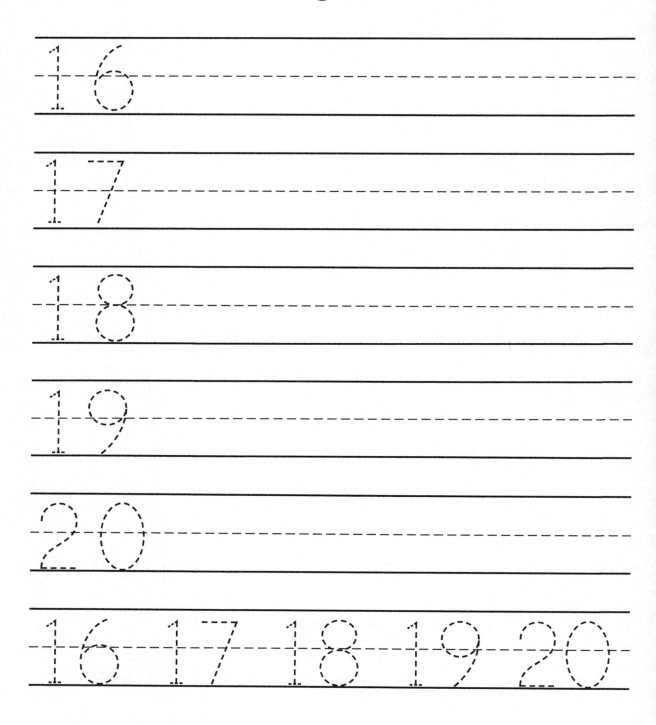

Big Book of Number Tracing: 0-100

Practice writing numbers 1-100.

Big Book of Number Tracing: 0-100

Practice writing numbers 1-100.

26

27

28

29

30

26 27 28 29 30

Big Book of Number Tracing: 0-100

Practice writing numbers 1-100.

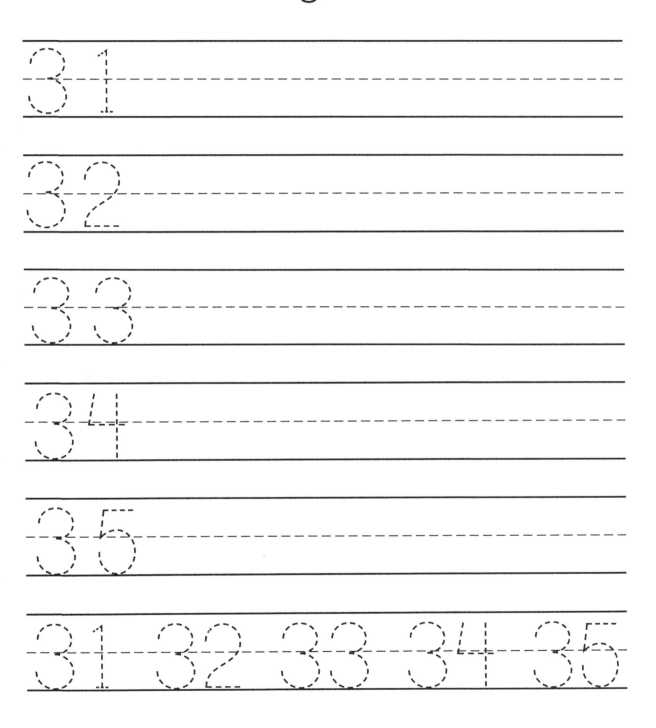

Big Book of Number Tracing: 0-100

Practice writing numbers 1-100.

36

37

38

39

40

36 37 38 39 40

Big Book of Number Tracing: 0-100

Practice writing numbers 1-100.

41

42

43

44

45

41 42 43 44 45

Big Book of Number Tracing: 0-100

Practice writing numbers 1-100.

46

47

48

49

50

46 47 48 49 50

Big Book of Number Tracing: 0-100

Practice writing numbers 1-100.

51

52

53

54

55

51 52 53 54 55

Big Book of Number Tracing: 0-100

Practice writing numbers 1-100.

56

57

58

59

60

56 57 58 59 60

Big Book of Number Tracing: 0-100

Practice writing numbers 1-100.

61

62

63

64

65

61 62 63 64 65

Big Book of Number Tracing: 0-100

Practice writing numbers 1-100.

Big Book of Number Tracing: 0-100

Practice writing numbers 1-100.

71

72

73

74

75

71 72 73 74 75

Big Book of Number Tracing: 0-100

Practice writing numbers 1-100.

76

77

78

79

80

76 77 78 79 80

Big Book of Number Tracing: 0-100

Practice writing numbers 1-100.

81

82

83

84

85

81 82 83 84 85

Big Book of Number Tracing: 0-100

Practice writing numbers 1-100.

86

87

88

89

90

86 87 88 89 90

Big Book of Number Tracing: 0-100

Practice writing numbers 1-100.

Big Book of Number Tracing: 0-100

Practice writing numbers 1-100.

96

97

98

99

100

96 97 98 99 100

Big Book of Number Tracing: 0-100

Made in the USA
Monee, IL
28 March 2021